How to Use This Literature Guide (cont.)

Vocabulary

Each teacher reference vocabulary overview page has definitions and sentences about how key vocabulary words are used in the section. These words should be introduced and discussed with students. Students will use these words in different activities throughout the book.

On some of the vocabulary student pages, students are asked to answer text-related questions about vocabulary words from the sections. The following question stems will help you create your own vocabulary questions if you'd like to extend the discussion.

- How does this word describe _____'s character?
- How does this word connect to the problem in this story?
- How does this word help you understand the setting?
- Tell me how this word connects to the main idea of this story.
- What visual pictures does this word bring to your mind?
- Why do you think the author used this word?

At times, you may find that more work with the words will help students understand their meanings and importance. These quick vocabulary activities are a good way to further study the words.

- Students can play vocabulary concentration. Make one set of cards that has the words on them and another set with the definitions. Then, have students lay them out on the table and play concentration. The goal of the game is to match vocabulary words with their definitions. For early readers or English language learners, the two sets of cards could be the words and pictures of the words.

- Students can create word journal entries about the words. Students choose words they think are important and then describe why they think each word is important within the book. Early readers or English language learners could instead draw pictures about the words in a journal.

- Students can create puppets and use them to act out the vocabulary words from the stories. Students may also enjoy telling their own character-driven stories using vocabulary words from the original stories.

How to Use This Literature Guide (cont.)

Analyzing the Literature

After you have read each section with students, hold a small-group or whole-class discussion. Provided on the teacher reference page for each section are leveled questions. The questions are written at two levels of complexity to allow you to decide which questions best meet the needs of your students. The Level 1 questions are typically less abstract than the Level 2 questions. These questions are focused on the various story elements, such as character, setting, and plot. Be sure to add further questions as your students discuss what they've read. For each question, a few key points are provided for your reference as you discuss the book with students.

Reader Response

In today's classrooms, there are often great readers who are below average writers. So much time and energy is spent in classrooms getting students to read on grade level that little time is left to focus on writing skills. To help teachers include more writing in their daily literacy instruction, each section of this guide has a literature-based reader response prompt. Each of the three genres of writing is used in the reader responses within this guide: narrative, informative/explanatory, and opinion. Before students write, you may want to allow them time to draw pictures related to the topic.

Guided Close Reading

Within each section of this guide, it is suggested that you closely reread a portion of the text with your students. Page numbers are given, but since some versions of the books may have different page numbers, the sections to be reread are described by location as well. After rereading the section, there are a few text-dependent questions to be answered by students.

Working space has been provided to help students prepare for the group discussion. They should record their thoughts and ideas on the activity page and refer to it during your discussion. Rather than just taking notes, you may want to require students to write complete responses to the questions before discussing them with you.

Encourage students to read one question at a time and then go back to the text and discover the answer. Work with students to ensure that they use the text to determine their answers rather than making unsupported inferences. Suggested answers are provided in the answer key.

How to Use This Literature Guide (cont.)

Guided Close Reading (cont.)

The generic open-ended stems below can be used to write your own text-dependent questions if you would like to give students more practice.

- What words in the story support . . . ?
- What text helps you understand . . . ?
- Use the book to tell why _____ happens.
- Based on the events in the story, . . . ?
- Show me the part in the text that supports . . . .
- Use the text to tell why . . . .

Making Connections

The activities in this section help students make cross-curricular connections to mathematics, science, social studies, fine arts, or other curricular areas. These activities require higher-order thinking skills from students but also allow for creative thinking.

Language Learning

A special section has been set aside to connect the literature to language conventions. Through these activities, students will have opportunities to practice the conventions of standard English grammar, usage, capitalization, and punctuation.

Story Elements

It is important to spend time discussing what the common story elements are in literature. Understanding the characters, setting, plot, and theme can increase students' comprehension and appreciation of the story. If teachers begin discussing these elements in early childhood, students will more likely internalize the concepts and look for the elements in their independent reading. Another very important reason for focusing on the story elements is that students will be better writers if they think about how the stories they read are constructed.

In the story elements activities, students are asked to create work related to the characters, setting, or plot. Consider having students complete only one of these activities. If you give students a choice on this assignment, each student can decide to complete the activity that most appeals to him or her. Different intelligences are used so that the activities are diverse and interesting to all students.

How to Use This Literature Guide *(cont.)*

Culminating Activity

At the end of this instructional guide is a creative culminating activity that allows students the opportunity to share what they've learned from reading the books in the series. This activity is open ended so that students can push themselves to create their own great works within your language arts classroom.

Comprehension Assessment

The questions in this section require students to think about the books they've read as well as the words that were used in the books. Some questions are tied to quotations from the books to engage students and require them to think about the text as they answer the questions.

Response to Literature

Finally, students are asked to respond to the literature by drawing pictures and writing about the characters and stories. A suggested rubric is provided for teacher reference.

Correlation to the Standards

Shell Education is committed to producing educational materials that are research and standards based. As part of this effort, we have correlated all of our products to the academic standards of all 50 states, the District of Columbia, the Department of Defense Dependents Schools, and all Canadian provinces.

Purpose and Intent of Standards

The Every Student Succeeds Act (ESSA) mandates that all states adopt challenging academic standards that help students meet the goal of college and career readiness. While many states already adopted academic standards prior to ESSA, the act continues to hold states accountable for detailed and comprehensive standards. Standards are statements that describe the criteria necessary for students to meet specific academic goals. They define the knowledge, skills, and content students should acquire at each level. State standards are used in the development of our products, so educators can be assured they meet state academic requirements.

How to Find Standards Correlations

To print a customized correlation report of this product for your state, visit our website at **www.teachercreatedmaterials.com/administrators/correlations/** and follow the online directions. If you require assistance in printing correlation reports, please contact our Customer Service Department at 1-877-777-3450.

Standards Correlation Chart

The lessons in this guide were written to support today's college and career readiness standards. This chart indicates which sections of this guide address which standards.

College and Career Readiness Standards	Section
Read closely to determine what the text says explicitly and to make logical inferences from it; cite specific textual evidence when writing or speaking to support conclusions drawn from the text.	Analyzing the Literature Sections 1–5; Guided Close Reading Sections 1–5; Story Elements Sections 1–5
Analyze how and why individuals, events, or ideas develop and interact over the course of a text.	Story Elements Sections 1–5; Guided Close Reading Sections 1–5
Interpret words and phrases as they are used in a text, including determining technical, connotative, and figurative meanings, and analyze how specific word choices shape meaning or tone.	Vocabulary Sections 1–5
Analyze the structure of texts, including how specific sentences, paragraphs, and larger portions of the text (e.g., a section, chapter, scene, or stanza) relate to each other and the whole.	Story Elements Sections 1–2
Read and comprehend complex literary and informational texts independently and proficiently.	Entire Unit
Write arguments to support claims in an analysis of substantive topics or texts using valid reasoning and relevant and sufficient evidence.	Reader Response Sections 2, 4
Write informative/explanatory texts to examine and convey complex ideas and information clearly and accurately through the effective selection, organization, and analysis of content.	Reader Response Sections 1, 5
Write narratives to develop real or imagined experiences or events using effective technique, well-chosen details and well-structured event sequences.	Reader Response Section 3
Produce clear and coherent writing in which the development, organization, and style are appropriate to task, purpose, and audience.	Reader Response Sections 1–5
Develop and strengthen writing as needed by planning, revising, editing, rewriting, or trying a new approach.	Story Elements Section 5
Conduct short as well as more sustained projects based on focused questions, demonstrating understanding of the subject under investigation.	Making Connections Sections 1, 3; Post-Reading Response to Literature
Demonstrate command of the conventions of standard English grammar and usage when writing or speaking.	Vocabulary Sections 1–5; Guided Close Reading Sections 1–5; Making Connections Section 1; Language Learning Sections 3–4; Story Elements Section 2; Post-Reading Response to Literature
Demonstrate command of the conventions of standard English capitalization, punctuation, and spelling when writing.	Reader Response Sections 1–5; Language Learning Sections 1, 5

College and Career Readiness Standards	Section
Apply knowledge of language to understand how language functions in different contexts, to make effective choices for meaning or style, and to comprehend more fully when reading or listening.	Guided Close Reading Sections 1–5
Determine or clarify the meaning of unknown and multiple-meaning words and phrases by using context clues, analyzing meaningful word parts, and consulting general and specialized reference materials, as appropriate.	Vocabulary Sections 1–5; Language Learning Section 2
Determine or clarify the meaning of unknown and multiple-meaning words and phrases by using context clues, analyzing meaningful word parts, and consulting general and specialized reference materials, as appropriate.	Vocabulary Sections 1–5
Demonstrate understanding of figurative language, word relationships, and nuances in word meanings.	Vocabulary Sections 4–5
Acquire and use accurately a range of general academic and domain-specific words and phrases sufficient for reading, writing, speaking, and listening at the college and career readiness level; demonstrate independence in gathering vocabulary knowledge when encountering an unknown term important to comprehension or expression.	Vocabulary Sections 1–5

TESOL and WIDA Standards

The lessons in this book promote English language development for English language learners. The following TESOL and WIDA English Language Development standards are addressed through the activities in this book:

- **Standard 1:** English language learners communicate for social and instructional purposes within the school setting.

- **Standard 2:** English language learners communicate information, ideas, and concepts necessary for academic success in the content area of language arts.

About the Author—Eleanor Estes

Eleanor Ruth Estes was born in West Haven, Connecticut, on May 9, 1906. She was one of four children born to Louis and Caroline Rosenfeld. Her father died when she was young, and her mother provided for the family as a dressmaker. Her mother was an excellent storyteller. In fact, Estes credited her love of reading and storytelling to her mother.

As a young adult, Estes worked at the New Haven Free Public Library. In 1931, she received a scholarship to study at the Pratt Institute Library School in Brooklyn, New York. It was there that she met and married her husband, Rice Estes. Both of them worked in New York libraries until 1941.

While living and working in New York, Estes became ill with tuberculosis and was bedridden. It was during this time that she began writing. She drew on memories from her childhood and her hometown in Connecticut. She turned these memories into several books.

Estes and her husband moved to the Los Angeles area for a time, where they had their first and only child, Helena. In 1952, the Estes family moved back to Connecticut. They lived there until Estes's death on July 15, 1988. She was 82 years old. She wrote 19 children's books, including *Ginger Pye*, which received the Newbery Medal. Three of her other books (*The Middle Moffat*, *Rufus M.*, and *The Hundred Dresses*) were Newbery Honor books.

Possible Texts for Text Comparisons

Estes has written a number of other books, including: The Moffats series, *Ginger Pye*, *The Witch Family*, and *Miranda the Great*, all of which would make for good comparisons.

Cross-Curricular Connection

This book would make an excellent introduction to immigration. Students could investigate the reasons people leave the countries they lived in, how they arrive in the new countries, and challenges they faced as immigrants. It can also be used within a character education unit on friendship, kindness, bullying, and speaking out against wrongs.

Book Summary of *The Hundred Dresses*

Every day, Peggy and Maddie wait for Wanda Petronski to play a game. Peggy teases Wanda by asking her about the hundred dresses she says she has at home. The other girls in the class don't believe it's true because Wanda wears the same faded blue dress to school each day. Maddie does not say anything but goes along with the game because she is not brave enough to stand up to Peggy.

One day, Wanda doesn't come to school. Her family has moved, and now Peggy and Maddie feel badly for how they treated Wanda. When their classroom teacher announces Wanda as the winner of a dress design contest and displays Wanda's designs of one hundred dresses, the girls decide to find Wanda to tell her about the award and to reconcile.

The girls walk to the area of town where Wanda and her family lived, but the Petronskis have already moved. The girls write Wanda a letter hoping that the post office will forward it, but they don't hear from Wanda immediately.

When their teacher finally receives a letter, Wanda is kind with her words, and she includes instructions that specific drawings be given to Peggy and Maddie. When Maddie and Peggy get home and look at the drawings closer, they realize that Wanda has drawn them. Both girls, and especially Maddie, learn a lesson about being kind from the very person they were being unkind to each day.

Possible Texts for Text Sets

- Blume, Judy. 2014. *Blubber*. New York: Atheneum Books for Young Readers.

- Cohen, Barbara. 2005. *Molly's Pilgrim*. New York: HarperCollins.

- Cooper, Scott. 2005. *Speak Up and Get Along! Learn the Mighty Might, Thought Chop, and More Tools to Make Friends, Stop Teasing, and Feel Good About Yourself*. Minneapolis: Free Spirit Publishing.

- Ludwig, Trudy. 2013. *The Invisible Boy*. New York: Knopf Books for Young Readers.

- McCloud, Carol. 2015. *Have You Filled a Bucket Today?: A Guide to Daily Happiness for Kids*. Brighton: Bucket Fillers.

- Michelle, Lonnie. 2002. *How Kids Make Friends: Secrets for Making Lots of Friends No Matter How Shy You Are*. Evenston: Freedom Publishing Company.

- O'Neill, Alexis. 2002. *The Recess Queen*. New York: Scholastic.

- Sornson, Bob. 2010. *The Juice Box Bully: Empowering Kids to Stand Up for Others*. Northville: FerrePress.

Pre-Reading Theme Thoughts

Directions: Draw a picture of a happy face or a sad face. Your face should show how you feel about each statement. Then, use words to say what you think about each statement.

Statement	How Do You Feel? 😊 ☹	Explain Your Answer
Your words do not affect other people.		
You are not a bully if you do not say anything.		
Sometimes, people have hidden talents.		
It is never too late to make things right.		

Vocabulary Overview

Key words and phrases from this section are provided below with definitions and sentences about how the words are used in the story. Introduce and discuss these important vocabulary words with students. If you think these words or other words in the story warrant more time devoted to them, there are suggestions in the introduction for other vocabulary activities (page 5).

Word	Definition	Sentence about Text
absence	not present	Wanda is **absent** from school.
usually	most of the time	Wanda **usually** sits at the back of the room.
marks	grades	The rough boys do not have good **marks**.
scuffling	move quickly	The rough boys **scuffle** their feet a lot.
roar	to make a loud sound	The boys **roar** with laughter.
contrary	opposite	**Contrary** to the boys, Wanda is not noisy.
rarely	not often	Wanda **rarely** speaks in class.
caked	covered	Wanda's feet are **caked** with mud.
apt	likely to happen	Some kids are **apt** to have dirty shoes every day.
auburn	reddish brown	Peggy has **auburn** hair.
unison	altogether	The class recites the Gettysburg Address in **unison**.

Vocabulary Activity

Directions: Read the phrases below. Replace the underlined words with vocabulary words. Use words from the Word Bank.

Word Bank

rarely	auburn	marks	caked
scuffling	in unison	apt	usually

1. <u>most of the time</u> sits in the corner _____

2. <u>movement</u> of feet _____

3. <u>covered</u> with dry mud _____

4. <u>reddish brown</u> hair _____

5. good <u>grades</u> on report cards _____

6. recited the Gettysburg Address <u>together</u> _____

7. <u>likely</u> to have dirty shoes _____

8. <u>almost never</u> said anything _____

Directions: Use one of the phrases in a complete sentence.

_____

_____

_____

Teacher Plans

Analyzing the Literature

Provided below are discussion questions you can use in small groups, with the whole class, or for written assignments. Each question is written at two levels so that you can choose the right question for each group of students. For each question, a few key points are provided for your reference as you discuss the book with students.

Story Element	Level 1	Level 2	Key Discussion Points
Setting	Describe the setting of this chapter.	How does the setting of this chapter relate to the characters?	The setting of the chapter is a classroom. The characters are all students in the classroom, so they are all classmates. Wanda is also a student of the class, but she is absent.
Character	How is Wanda described?	What evidence is there to support the idea that the other students did not notice Wanda when she was at school?	Wanda is described as quiet. She sits in the corner of the room. The text states that nobody thought about her in class, but they did wait for her at lunchtime to "have fun with her." It takes several days for students to notice that she has been absent.
Character	Who sits in the corner of the room?	Describe the boys who sit in the corner.	The rough boys sit in the corner of the room. They do not get good marks. The corner of the room is described as being noisier than the rest of the class. The boys in the corner scuffle their feet and laugh a lot. That area of the room is also described as having mud and dirt on the floor.
Plot	When do Peggy and Maddie notice Wanda has been absent?	What event makes Peggy and Maddie notice that Wanda has been absent?	Peggy and Maddie wait for Wanda one morning on their way to school so they can "have fun with her." They are late getting to class because they keep waiting even though Wanda doesn't come.

Reader Response

Think

In "Wanda," several different types of students are described. Think about what kind of student you are.

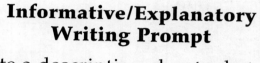

Informative/Explanatory Writing Prompt

Write a description about what kind of student you are. Tell about how you behave, where you sit, and how you act with your classmates.

Name _____ Date _____

Guided Close Reading

Closely reread the description of where Wanda sits. Start at the beginning of the chapter. End with, "but that was all."

Directions: Think about these questions. In the space below, write ideas or draw pictures as you think. Be ready to share your answers.

❶ How is Wanda's behavior described?

❷ What evidence is there for why Wanda's feet are so dirty?

❸ What possible reason is given as to why Wanda sits in the corner?

Making Connections–The Gettysburg Address

Directions: Read the text. Then, answer the questions below.

> President Abraham Lincoln gave a well-known speech. He gave the speech after the Battle of Gettysburg. It was given in 1863. The United States was in the middle of the Civil War. Two parts of the country were fighting. In the speech, Lincoln calls for the country to stay together. The first sentence of the speech is famous even today!

1. What is the Gettysburg Address?

_____

_____

_____

2. What was happening in the United States that made Lincoln ask the country to stay together?

_____

_____

_____

_____

Challenge: Memorize either the first sentence of the Gettysburg Address or the portion of the address that is featured in the chapter "Wanda."

Name _____ Date _____

Language Learning–Contractions

Directions: Write the two words each contraction is made up of. The first one has been done for you.

Language Hints!

Contractions are words put together to make new words. Letters are taken out. They are replaced with an apostrophe.

1. didn't = _____ *did* _____ + _____ *not* _____

2. wasn't = _____ + _____

3. she'd = _____ + _____

4. isn't = _____ + _____

5. we'd = _____ + _____

6. they'd = _____ + _____

Directions: Write a sentence using at least two of the contractions above.

_____

_____

_____

_____

Story Elements-Characters

Directions: Fill in the Venn diagram with information about each of the characters.

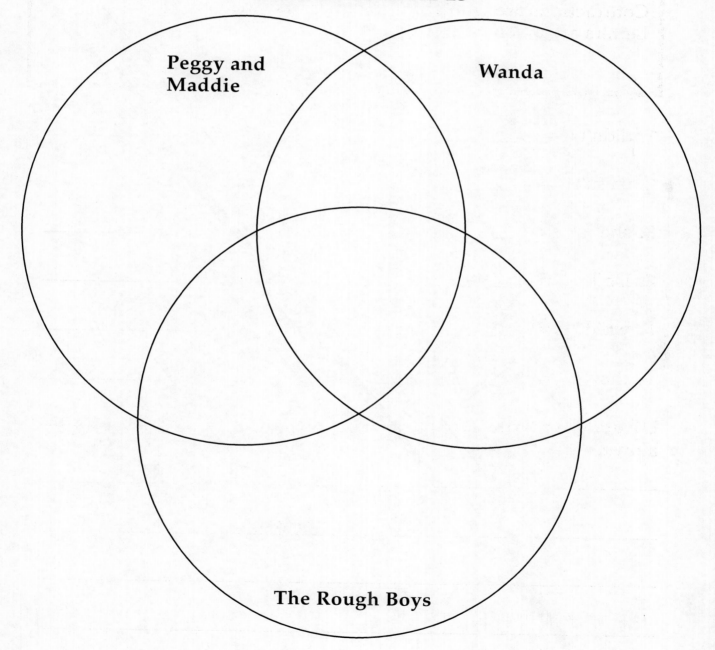

Students in Room 13

Peggy and
Maddie

Wanda

The Rough Boys

Story Elements–Plot

Directions: Think about who notices that Wanda is absent. Then, complete the time line to show in what order they notice.

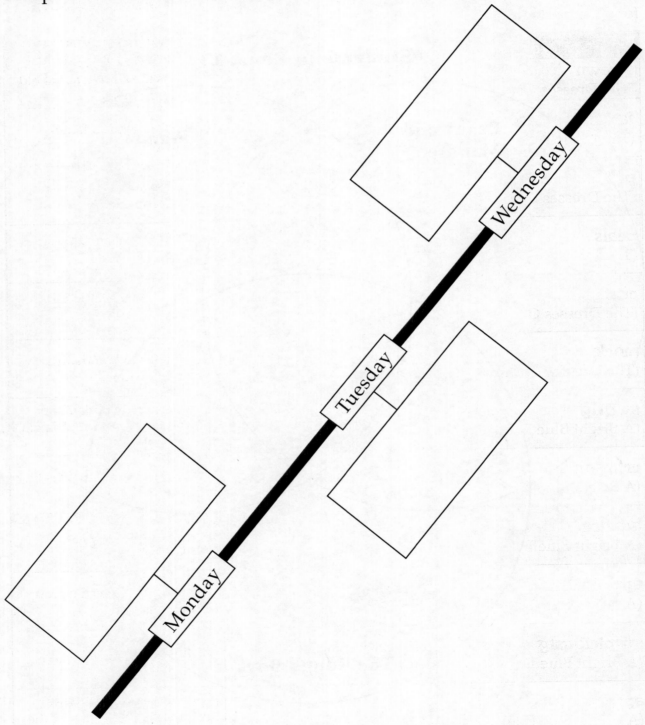

Vocabulary Overview

Key words and phrases from this section are provided below with definitions and sentences about how the words are used in the story. Introduce and discuss these important vocabulary words with students. If you think these words or other words in the story warrant more time devoted to them, there are suggestions in the introduction for other vocabulary activities (page 5).

Word	Definition	Sentence about Text
strewn (The Dresses Game)	spread out; scattered	Tin cans are **strewn** about old man Svenson's yard.
faded (The Dresses Game)	less bright in color	Wanda's dress is a **faded** blue color.
properly (The Dresses Game)	done correctly according to rules; appropriately	Wanda's dress is not ironed **properly**.
peals (The Dresses Game)	many loud sounds	The girls burst into **peals** of laughter.
cruel (The Dresses Game)	mean	Peggy does not think she is **cruel**.
mock (The Dresses Game)	fake	Peggy talks to Wanda in a **mock** polite tone.
swiftly (A Bright Blue Day)	quickly; fast	Maddie **swiftly** remembers the day the game with Wanda began.
crimson (A Bright Blue Day)	deep red color	The **crimson** dress catches the sun's light.
admire (A Bright Blue Day)	think highly of	All the girls **admire** Cecile's dress.
approached (A Bright Blue Day)	came close to	Wanda **approaches** the group of girls.
suspiciously (A Bright Blue Day)	feeling that something is wrong	The girls look at Wanda **suspiciously**.
approving (A Bright Blue Day)	accepting	Peggy teases Wanda to hear the **approving** laughter of the other girls.

Name _____ Date _____

Vocabulary Activity

Directions: Review the words and definitions. Then, answer the questions.

1. **swiftly**—quickly; fast

   What is something you do **swiftly**?

   _____

   _____

2. **crimson**—deep red color

   Look around the room. What is something you see that is **crimson**?

   _____

   _____

3. **admire**—think highly of

   Who is someone you **admire**?

   _____

   _____

4. **properly**—done correctly according to rules; appropriately

   What is something you do **properly**?

   _____

   _____

Analyzing the Literature

Provided below are discussion questions you can use in small groups, with the whole class, or for written assignments. Each question is written at two levels so that you can choose the right question for each group of students. For each question, a few key points are provided for your reference as you discuss the book with students.

Story Element	Level 1	Level 2	Key Discussion Points
Character	How is Wanda described in the chapter "The Dresses Game"?	Why do you think Peggy and Maddie want to "have fun" with Wanda?	Wanda is described as having a funny last name and living in a place where people do not want to live, Boggins Heights. She does not have any friends and walks to and from school alone. She wears the same wrinkled, faded blue dress every day. Because of the way Wanda is described, it can be inferred that Peggy and Maddie likely "have fun" with Wanda because they think she is different from them and the other students in the class.
Setting	How is Boggins Heights described?	How is the setting related to Wanda's character?	Boggins Heights is described as a place people do not want to live. Old man Svenson, a man who lives there, is described as "no good." His house is described as messy. This relates to Wanda because it shows that she is from a less desirable part of town. Wanda is an easy target because she lives in a poor area.
Plot	What happens after Wanda says she has one hundred dresses?	What happens as a result of Wanda telling the girls she has one hundred dresses?	After Wanda says she has one hundred dresses, the other girls stop playing to listen to the conversation and laugh. Peggy and Maddie begin waiting for Wanda each day to ask her, in a mocking way, about the hundred dresses she has. They also provoke her to describe the shoes and hats she has, too.
Character	How is the group of girls described?	What is the response of the group of girls to the dresses game that Peggy begins?	The girls are more interested in the dresses they have and the ones they want to get than they are Wanda's feelings. The game begins so quickly that everybody just goes along with it. Maddie, especially, wishes they would stop teasing Wanda.

Name _____ Date _____

Reader Response

Think

Maddie is sympathetic to Wanda but is too scared to speak up to Peggy, so she goes along with the dresses game.

Opinion Writing Prompt

Do you think Maddie has good reasons for not speaking up to Peggy about the dresses game? Tell your opinion. Use details to support your answer.

_____

_____

_____

_____

_____

_____

_____

_____

_____

Guided Close Reading

Closely reread the section at the end of "The Dresses Game" where Maddie's reaction to the game is described. Begin with, "As for Maddie...." Continue through the end of the chapter.

Directions: Think about these questions. In the space below, write ideas or draw pictures as you think. Be ready to share your answers.

❶ How does Maddie feel about the game Peggy is playing every day with Wanda?

❷ What does Maddie do while Peggy is questioning Wanda?

❸ Why does Maddie not speak out against what Peggy is doing?

Name _____ Date _____

Making Connections–October Weather

Directions: It is October on the day the dresses game begins. Draw a picture of how the weather is described on that October day. Then, draw a picture of what the weather is like in October where you live.

October in the Book

October Where I Live

Language Learning–Affixes and Root Words

Directions: The affixes *in–*, *im–*, *un–*, and *dis–* can all mean "not" or "the opposite of." In the left column, underline the affix in each word. Then, match each word to its meaning.

inseparable	not comfortable
impatient	not what is expected
unexpected	not able to separate
uncomfortable	not patient

Directions: Answer the question.

1. What does the word *disorganized* mean?

_____

_____

Story Elements–Plot

Directions: Fill in the events that lead up to the dresses game. Use the text to help you.

> The girls admire Cecile's new dress.

⬇

> [blank]

⬇

> [blank]

⬇

> The girls laugh and make fun of what Wanda has said.

⬇

> [blank]

Story Elements–Character

Directions: Reread this section of the text with the characters in mind. Write a sentence from the text that best explains each character's personality.

Character	Sentence from Text
Wanda	
Peggy	
Maddie	
the other girls	

Vocabulary Overview

Key words and phrases from this section are provided below with definitions and sentences about how the words are used in the story. Introduce and discuss these important vocabulary words with students. If you think these words or other words in the story warrant more time devoted to them, there are suggestions in the introduction for other vocabulary activities (page 5).

Word	Definition	Sentence about Text
disguise (The Contest)	change the appearance of	Maddie tries to **disguise** the dresses she gets from Peggy.
trimmings (The Contest)	additional items added to decorate something	Maddie's mother puts new **trimmings** on Peggy's old dresses.
recognize (The Contest)	know and remember something because of prior knowledge	Maddie hopes the other girls do not **recognize** the dresses Peggy gives her.
brilliant (The Contest)	bright or impressive	The dresses Wanda draws are **brilliant**.
lavish (The Hundred Dresses)	rich and expensive quality	Wanda draws dresses with **lavish** designs.
admiringly (The Hundred Dresses)	with respect and enjoyment	The class **admiringly** looks at Wanda's drawings.
exhibition (The Hundred Dresses)	display of something in a public place	Wanda's drawings are on **exhibition** in the classroom.
deliberately (The Hundred Dresses)	done on purpose	The teacher hopes nobody **deliberately** hurt Wanda's feelings.
coward (The Hundred Dresses)	someone who is afraid to do what is right	Maddie feels like a **coward** for not standing up for Wanda.
miserable (The Hundred Dresses)	unhappy	Peggy makes Wanda's life **miserable** by teasing her.

Vocabulary Activity

Directions: Sort the vocabulary words into the parts of speech chart.

Word Bank

disguise	lavish	trimmings	exhibition
miserable	recognize	brilliant	coward

Nouns	Verbs	Adjectives

Directions: Answer this question.

1. Why does Maddie's mom **disguise** her dresses with **trimmings**?

_____

_____

_____

Analyzing the Literature

Provided below are discussion questions you can use in small groups, with the whole class, or for written assignments. Each question is written at two levels so that you can choose the right question for each group of students. For each question, a few key points are provided for your reference as you discuss the book with students.

Story Element	Level 1	Level 2	Key Discussion Points
Plot	What does Maddie worry about now that Wanda is gone?	Why is Maddie worried Peggy will make fun of her now that Wanda is gone?	Maddie is worried that Peggy will make fun of her dresses now that Wanda is gone. Maddie's dresses have been handed down to her from Peggy. Maddie's mother has added trimmings to the dresses to try to disguise them so that the other girls will not recognize them, but Maddie is worried the other girls might notice.
Setting	What is displayed in the classroom when Maddie and Peggy walk in?	Why are Maddie and Peggy amazed when they walk into the classroom?	The teacher displays Wanda's hundred dress designs throughout the classroom. The girls are amazed when they walk in because they see Wanda's designs displayed in every part of the room. The girls all stop and gasp at how beautiful the designs are.
Character	What does the letter from Mr. Petronski tell about Wanda's family?	What can we learn from the way Mr. Petronski's letter is written?	Mr. Petronski's letter indicates that they are moving to a big city so that the family will not be made fun of anymore. He states there are many funny names in the big city. The language he uses indicates that he is Polish and that he does not speak standard English fluently.
Character	How does Maddie react to the letter from Mr. Petronski?	Explain why Maddie reacts the way she does to Mr. Petronski's letter.	Maddie has a difficult time concentrating on her schoolwork after the letter is read. She feels badly for the way she stood by and said nothing while Peggy teased Wanda.

Reader Response

Think

Maddie is afraid of Peggy. She does not want to stand up to Peggy when she teases Wanda. Maddie is afraid Peggy will begin teasing her when Wanda is gone. Think about how friends should treat each other.

Narrative Writing Prompt

Write about a time when one of your friends stood up for you or when you stood up for a friend. How did it make you feel?

_____

_____

_____

_____

_____

_____

_____

_____

_____

_____

Name _____ Date _____

Guided Close Reading

Closely reread the section where Maddie cannot concentrate on her lessons. Begin with, "The first period...." Continue through the end of the chapter.

Directions: Think about these questions. In the space below, write ideas or draw pictures as you think. Be ready to share your answers.

❶ Why can't Maddie put her mind on her work?

❷ Based on the book, why does Maddie say she was a coward?

❸ How does Maddie decide to make things right?

Name _____ Date _____

Making Connections–Immigration

Directions: We learn in his letter that Mr. Petronski is from Poland. People in America come from all over the world. Survey your class to find out where their families came from. Make a tally graph to show the places your classmates' families are from.

North America	
South America	
Africa	
Asia	
Australia	
Europe	

Directions: Answer this question.

1. Look at your tally marks. What do they tell you?

_____

_____

Name _____ Date _____

Language Learning–Adverbs

Directions: There are many adverbs in the chapter "The Hundred Dresses." Find five sentences in the chapter that use adverbs. Write the sentences in the chart. Underline the adverbs. Then, write the verbs the adverbs describe. An example has been done for you.

Language Hints!

Adverbs are words that describe verbs. They often end with *–ly*.

Sentence with Adverb	Verb the Adverb Describes
"Do you think Miss Mason will <u>surely</u> announce the winners today?" asked Peggy.	announce

Story Elements–Character

Directions: Write a short summary of each character's role in the dress game.

Wanda	
Peggy	
Maddie	

Name _____ Date _____

Story Elements-Setting

Directions: Much of the beginning of the "The Hundred Dresses" chapter is spent describing what the classroom looks like with the dress designs hanging around the room. Draw the setting based on how it is described in the text.

Vocabulary Overview

Key words and phrases from this section are provided below with definitions and sentences about how the words are used in the story. Introduce and discuss these important vocabulary words with students. If you think these words or other words in the story warrant more time devoted to them, there are suggestions in the introduction for other vocabulary activities (page 5).

Word	Definition	Sentence about Text
dismal	gloomy; dreary	The November afternoon is damp and **dismal**.
assailed	attacked or criticized	Maddie imagines she **assails** anyone who picks on Wanda.
drab	plain	Boggins Heights is **drab** and cold.
sparse	smaller than normal; thin	The Petronskis have a **sparse** little yard.
amends	compensaton for a wrong doing	Maddie wants to make **amends** with Wanda.
frail	weak or without strength	The Petronskis' front door is **frail** and does not give much protection against the cold and wind.
dilapidated	in bad condition because of age or lack of care	The cat is hiding under old man Svenson's **dilapidated** wood chair.
unintelligible	unable to be understood	When old man Svenson does respond to the girls, his words are **unintelligible**.
disconsolate	very unhappy; sad	Maddie and Peggy feel **disconsolate** when they are looking for Wanda.
conclusion	final decision after a period of thought	Maddie comes to the **conclusion** that she will stand up for people.

Name _____ Date _____

Vocabulary Activity

Directions: Choose five vocabulary words that are difficult for you. Fill in the chart below to help you learn the words better.

Word	Definition	Synonyms or other words that remind you of the word

Analyzing the Literature

Provided below are discussion questions you can use in small groups, with the whole class, or for written assignments. Each question is written at two levels so that you can choose the right question for each group of students. For each question, a few key points are provided for your reference as you discuss the book with students.

Story Element	Level 1	Level 2	Key Discussion Points
Character	What comment does Peggy make about Wanda when she is on her way to Boggins Heights?	Peggy says, "I never thought she had the sense to know we were making fun of her anyway." What does the use of the word *we* tell about Peggy?	Peggy makes a comment to Maddie that she didn't call Wanda a foreigner or funny names. Peggy also says that she thought Wanda was too dumb to know that they were making fun of her. Peggy uses the word *we* to indicate that she thought she was not the only one who was making fun of Wanda.
Setting	How does the author describe Boggins Heights?	What evidence does the author provide that Boggins Heights is drab, cold, and cheerless?	The author states that Boggins Heights is drab, cold, and cheerless. The brook is just a trickle; there is trash, such as tin cans, old shoes, and broken umbrellas, in the brook.
Plot	In what ways does Maddie look for hope that Wanda and her family have not moved?	Maddie looks for any hope that Wanda and her family have not yet moved. What does this tell about Maddie?	Maddie suggests that maybe the Petronskis just went away for a little while and will be back. When she sees the cat, she hopes the cat is theirs, too, and that they will come back for it. Maddie really wants to make amends with Wanda and is saddened that she may not be able to.
Plot	How does Peggy react to not being able to find Wanda?	Describe the difference in how Maddie and Peggy each react to not being able to find Wanda.	Peggy is satisfied that they tried and states, "What can we do?" as if there is nothing more to be done. She suggests that asking Wanda about her dresses was giving her ideas for her drawings. Maddie is very upset that Wanda is gone and that she is not able to make amends. Maddie decides that she is no longer going to stand by while someone else is being picked on.

Name _____ Date _____

Reader Response

Think

At the end of the chapter, Maddie decides she is no longer going to stand by. She is not going to allow people to be picked on. Think about whether this would be easy or hard to do.

Opinion Writing Prompt

Write about whether or not it is easy to stand up and do the right thing when someone else is doing the wrong thing. Include an introduction stating your opinion, a few supporting details, and a conclusion.

_____

_____

_____

_____

_____

_____

_____

_____

Guided Close Reading

Closely reread the section where Maddie is in her bed doing "hard thinking."

Directions: Think about these questions. In the space below, write ideas or draw pictures as you think. Be ready to share your answers.

❶ What conclusion does Maddie come to after doing some hard thinking?

❷ What other reasons does Maddie think of for why kids are picked on at her school?

❸ What consequences is Maddie willing to face if she stands up for someone being picked on?

Name _____ Date _____

Making Connections–Land Features

Directions: "Up on Boggins Heights" refers to several land features. Fill in the chart with information about each land feature.

Land Feature	Definition	Illustration
hill		
brook		
woods		

Language Learning–Adjectives

Directions: Draw a line to match each noun with the two adjectives that describe it.

Language Hints!

Adjectives are describing words. They describe nouns.

1. the afternoon   drab and cheerless

2. Boggins Heights   damp and dismal

3. the cat   yellow and timid

4. the chair   yellow and tangled

5. old man Svenson's hair   dilapidated and wooden

Directions: Write two adjectives to describe Maddie.

_____   _____

Name _____ Date _____

Story Elements—Character and Setting

Directions: Draw a picture of old man Svenson and his house using the description in this chapter.

Story Elements–Character

Directions: Maddie and Peggy react very differently to not being able to find Wanda. Write a few key details from the text to show how each girl reacts.

Peggy	Maddie

Vocabulary Overview

Key words and phrases from this section are provided below with definitions and sentences about how the words are used in the story. Introduce and discuss these important vocabulary words with students. If you think these words or other words in the story warrant more time devoted to them, there are suggestions in the introduction for other vocabulary activities (page 5).

Word	Definition	Sentence about Text
ashamed	feeling of shame or guilt	Maddie imagines the girls feeling **ashamed** after she confronts them about picking on Wanda.
dull	not interesting; plain	Maddie imagines Wanda's eyes having a **dull** pain to them.
autumn	the season between summer and winter; fall	Cecile dances a dance called the "Passing of **Autumn**."
sudden	quick	The class has a **sudden** interest in hearing the letter from Wanda.
equalize	make or become equal	Wanda's new teacher does not **equalize** with Miss Mason.
relieved	happy because something difficult has been stopped	Peggy is **relieved** after hearing Wanda's letter read aloud.
brilliancy	brightness	Wanda's dress designs have **brilliancy** of color.
hastily	hurriedly	Maddie **hastily** rubs her eyes as she studies the dress design.
intently	done with aim or purpose	Maddie studies the dress design **intently**.
stolidly	without emotion	Wanda looks **stolidly** at the group of girls that laughed at her.

Vocabulary Activity

Directions: Cut apart the cards. Have one student select a card and act out the word. Other students try to guess what the word is.

ashamed

hastily

relieved

dull

sudden

intently

Teacher Note: You may wish to write the words on a chart paper or give each student a copy of this page, so they have access to the words.

Analyzing the Literature

Provided below are discussion questions you can use in small groups, with the whole class, or for written assignments. Each question is written at two levels so that you can choose the right question for each group of students. For each question, a few key points are provided for your reference as you discuss the book with students.

Story Element	Level 1	Level 2	Key Discussion Points
Character	How does Maddie feel about not being able to make things right with Wanda?	What evidence is there that Maddie cannot forget about how the girls made Wanda feel?	Maddie continues to think about Wanda, even after she and Peggy mail a letter to Wanda. Maddie even puts herself to sleep at night by making up speeches defending anyone who might tease Wanda. She also continues to feel sad.
Character	What does the text say about Wanda not having a mother?	What do Maddie and Peggy realize when they think about Wanda not having a mother?	The text states that the girls realized that Wanda doesn't have a mother, but they do not think about what that means for Wanda. After thinking about it, they realize that Wanda has to do her own washing and ironing. They also realize that since Wanda only has one blue dress, she probably has to do it at night after school.
Plot	What does Wanda's letter say to the class?	What does the content of Wanda's letter tell about her character?	Wanda writes to the class to tell them they can keep the hundred dresses designs. She gives specific designs to Peggy and Maddie for Christmas. She tells Miss Mason that she is better than her new teacher. She also wishes everyone a Merry Christmas. Wanda is not mean or vindictive in her letter. She is kind and giving, despite how the girls treated her.
Plot	What does Peggy think after seeing the faces on Wanda's drawings?	What evidence is there that Maddie does not have the same feelings Peggy does after seeing the faces on the drawings?	Wanda uses Peggy's and Maddie's faces on her drawings. Peggy thinks this shows how much Wanda liked them. Maddie agrees with Peggy verbally; however, she gets teary-eyed every time she thinks of the girls teasing Wanda about the hundred dresses.

Name _____ **Date** _____

Reader Response

Think

Maddie did not stand up to the girls teasing Wanda. Now, Maddie imagines herself standing up to anyone teasing Wanda. Think about how Maddie describes what she would do.

Expository/Informative Writing Prompt

Describe what you would do to stand up for someone who was being teased. Include an introduction, a few details, and a conclusion.

_____

_____

_____

_____

_____

_____

_____

_____

_____

_____

_____

Name _____ Date _____

Guided Close Reading

Closely reread the section when Maddie takes Wanda's drawing home and looks at it in her bedroom. Begin with, "She went home...." Stop with, "she ran over to Peggy's."

Directions: Think about these questions. In the space below, write ideas or draw pictures as you think. Be ready to share your answers.

❶ Why doesn't Maddie notice the face in the drawing at first?

❷ How does Maddie know it is her face in the drawing?

❸ What evidence is there that Maddie is excited about the gift Wanda has given to the girls?

Making Connections-The Christmas Season

Directions: This section of the text takes place at Christmastime. Reread the text for evidence of the Christmas season. Draw a picture about what you read.

Name _____ Date _____

Language Learning–Punctuation

Directions: Find a sentence from the chapter for each type of punctuation. Write each example in the chart.

Punctuation	Sentence from the Chapter
period (.)	
question mark (?)	
exclamation mark (!)	
quotation marks (" ")	
ellipsis (...)	
comma (,)	
apostrophe (')	

Name _____ **Date** _____

Story Elements-Setting

Directions: The setting changes several times in this chapter. Write about or draw four different settings from this chapter.

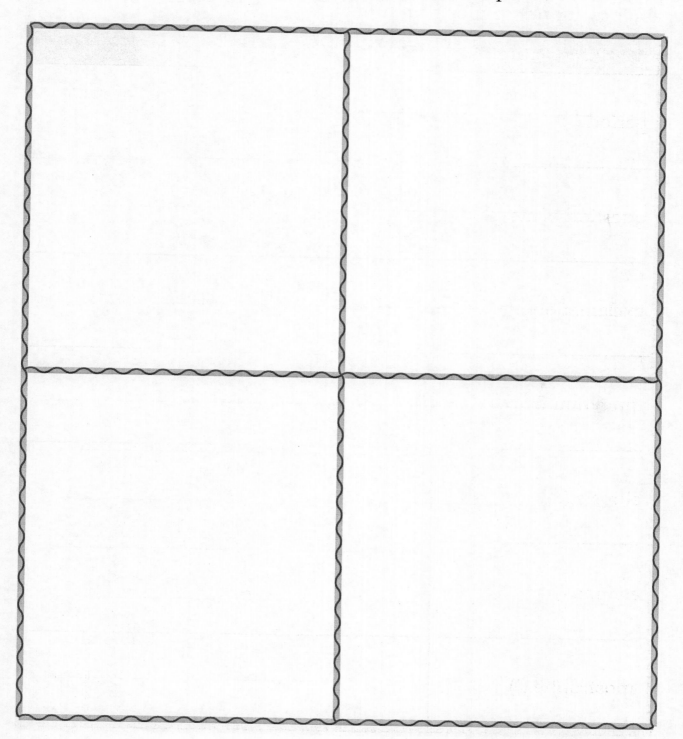

Story Elements-Character

Directions: Write a friendly letter to Wanda from Maddie. Include Maddie's true feelings for how they treated Wanda. Also include an apology for not standing up for her.

_____

_____

_____

_____

_____

_____

_____

_____

_____

_____

Sincerely,

_____

Name _____ Date _____

Post-Reading Theme Thoughts

Directions: Choose a main character from *The Hundred Dresses*. Pretend you are that character. Draw a picture of a happy face or a sad face to show how the character would feel about each statement. Then, use words to explain your picture.

Character I Chose: _____

Statement	How Do You Feel? 😊 ☹️	Explain Your Answer
Your words do not affect other people.		
You are not a bully if you do not say anything.		
Sometimes, people have hidden talents.		
It is never too late to make things right.		

Culminating Activity: Friendship Festival

Directions: Host a Friendship Festival in the classroom by using some or all of the suggestions below.

Dress Decorations

Celebrate the lessons learned in *The Hundred Dresses* by using students' dress designs from the Response to Literature section (page 67). Attempt to gather one hundred dresses by having students create multiple designs. Hang the dress designs around the room on the day of the Friendship Festival.

Friendship Soup

Invite each student to bring a can of soup. Combine the soups together for a fun snack that can be shared with friends at the Friendship Festival.

Friendship Flower

Combine construction paper hands to create a class friendship flower. Display the flower at the Friendship Festival.

Friendship Bingo

Play "Friendship Bingo." Photocopy the bingo card on page 63, and give one copy to each student. Allow students time to find classmates who can sign each of the boxes. Each student may only sign each card one time, even if he or she may be able to sign more than once. Continue to play until every student has all the boxes signed. Gather the class back together, and discuss which students signed each box to learn more about students.

Kindness Notes

Make copies of the *Kindness Notes* on page 64. Provide each student with two notes. Place each student's name in a basket two times. Have each student draw two names from the basket and write a kind note to each of the students whose names were drawn. (You may wish to do this ahead of time of the Friendship Festival in order to preview each note.) Distribute each note during the Friendship Festival.

Culminating Activity: Friendship Festival (cont.)

Friendship Soup

Directions: Share a snack with friends! Follow the instructions to create a unique and tasty soup to share during the Friendship Festival.

Materials

Provide the materials or ask parents for donations.

- bowls (1 per student)
- spoons (1 per student)
- napkins
- crackers (optional)
- juice boxes (optional)
- slow cooker
- large serving spoon

Instructions

1. Pour all the soups together into the slow cooker.

2. Tell students to stir in friendship by allowing each student to stir the pot four times. The first three times, he/she should think of the name of close friends. The fourth stir should be "all the boys and girls in the classroom."

3. Allow the soup to cook on high for 1½ – 2 hours. Stir occasionally.

4. Serve each child soup in a bowl with some crackers and a juice box, if desired.

Culminating Activity: Friendship Festival *(cont.)*

Friendship Flower

Directions: Follow these instructions to make a friendship flower to display at the Friendship Festival.

Materials:

- $\frac{1}{2}$ sheet of construction paper in various colors (one per student)
- scissors
- glue
- poster board or chart paper

Instructions

1. Provide each child with a $\frac{1}{2}$ sheet of construction paper.

2. Have each student trace his or her handprint on the construction paper and then cut it out.

3. Draw the stem of a flower on the poster board, leaving room at the top for the flower. Arrange the handprints in a circle around the top of the stem to form a large flower. Title the poster board with a friendship title such as "Friendship Flower," "We All Bloom Together," or "Flower of Friendship."

4. Display the flower in the classroom as a reminder of friendship.

Culminating Activity: Friendship Festival *(cont.)*

Friendship Bingo

Directions: Find a classmate for each box. Each classmate can only sign your card one time.

I like baseball.	I write letters to other people.	I like to cook.	I speak another language.
I have traveled to another country.	I am an only child.	I love Chinese food.	I have a last name with more than 6 letters. **>6**
I love animals.	I love Christmastime.	I draw well.	I have a brother.
I have a last name with less than 6 letters. **<6**	I love to read.	I have a sister.	I know how to swim.

Culminating Activity: Friendship Festival *(cont.)*

Kindness Note

To: _____

From: _____

_____

_____

_____

_____

Kindness Note

To: _____

From: _____

_____

_____

_____

_____

Name _____ Date _____

Comprehension Assessment

Directions: Fill in the bubble for the best response to each question.

Section 1: Wanda

1. What makes Peggy and Maddie finally realize that Wanda isn't coming to school?

   (A) They see that Wanda's seat is empty.

   (B) They see Wanda on the way to school.

   (C) They wait for Wanda, but she never comes.

   (D) Wanda isn't at school.

Section 2: The Dresses Game & A Bright Blue Day

2. How do Maddie and Peggy describe the fun they like to have with Wanda?

   (A) They play games with Wanda on the playground.

   (B) They play a game called "the dresses game."

   (C) They play with Wanda after school.

   (D) They do not play games with Wanda.

Section 3: The Contest & The Hundred Dresses

3. What does Maddie realize when she states, "'Look, Peg ... there's that blue one she told us about. Isn't it beautiful?'" as Maddie and Peggy are looking at the dress designs hanging in the classroom?

   (A) The designs are the dresses that Wanda was talking about.

   (B) The designs are the real dresses Wanda has at her house.

   (C) The designs could not have all been made by one person.

   (D) The designs are of the dresses they are wearing.

Comprehension Assessment (cont.)

Section 4: Up on Boggins Heights

4. Describe the lesson Maddie learns in this chapter.

_____

_____

_____

_____

_____

_____

_____

_____

Section 5: The Letter to Room 13

5. What does Maddie realize about the drawings Wanda gave to her and Peggy?

(A) Wanda wants Maddie and Peggy to have all the hundred dresses drawings.

(B) The faces in the drawings are of the two girls.

(C) Wanda knows that Maddie and Peggy like the dress designs in the drawings.

(D) The dresses in the drawings look like dresses that Maddie and Peggy had worn.

Response to Literature: Designing Dresses–Easy or Difficult?

Directions: Design a dress like Wanda does. Use the illustration of the dresses hanging in the classroom in the chapter "The Hundred Dresses" for inspiration.

Response to Literature:
Designing Dresses–Easy or Difficult? *(cont.)*

Directions: Use your drawing on page 67 and what you know about the book *The Hundred Dresses* to help you answer the questions.

1. Was it easy or difficult for Wanda to draw one hundred dress designs? What makes you think so?

_____

_____

_____

_____

2. Was it easy or difficult for you to draw a dress design? If it was difficult for you, what is something that comes more easily?

_____

_____

_____

_____

3. Why is it good that different people have different talents?

_____

_____

_____

Name _____ Date _____

Response to Literature Rubric

Directions: Use this rubric to evaluate student responses.

Great Job	Good Work	Keep Trying
☐ You answered all three questions completely. You included many details.	☐ You answered all three questions.	☐ You did not answer all three questions.
☐ Your handwriting is very neat. There are no spelling errors.	☐ Your handwriting can be neater. There are some spelling errors.	☐ Your handwriting is not very neat. There are many spelling errors.
☐ Your picture is neat and fully colored.	☐ Your picture is neat and some of it is colored.	☐ Your picture is not very neat and/or fully colored.
☐ Creativity is clear in both the picture and the writing.	☐ Creativity is clear in either the picture or the writing.	☐ There is not much creativity in either the picture or the writing.

Teacher Comments: _____

_____

_____

_____

Answer Key

The responses provided here are just examples of what students may answer. Many accurate responses are possible for the questions throughout this unit.

Vocabulary Activity—Section 1:
Wanda (page 15)
1. usually
2. scuffling
3. caked
4. auburn
5. marks
6. unison
7. apt
8. rarely

Guided Close Reading—Section 1:
Wanda (page 18)
1. Wanda is described as a quiet girl who "rarely said anything at all." The text says that no one has even heard her laugh out loud.
2. Wanda's feet are usually caked with dried mud because she has to walk on country roads to get to school.
3. The text speculates that the teacher keeps the children with dirty shoes in the corner of the room.

Making Connections—Section 1:
Wanda (page 19)
1. The Gettysburg Address is a speech given by Abraham Lincoln at a cemetery in Gettysburg, Pennsylvania.
2. The country was at war with itself during the Civil War.

Language Learning—Section 1:
Wanda (page 20)
1. did + not
2. was + not
3. she + did/would
4. is + not
5. we + did/would
6. they + did/would

Story Elements—Section 1:
Wanda (page 21)
Possible answers can include:
- **Peggy and Maddie**—get good grades/marks; sit in the front of the classroom
- **The Rough Boys**—do not get good grades/marks; sit in the corner of the room; make a lot of noise; dirty feet
- **Wanda**—is very quiet; has dirty feet; absent

Story Elements—Section 1:
Wanda (page 22)
- **Monday**—The text says that nobody noticed that Wanda is absent on Monday.
- **Tuesday**—The text says that nobody noticed, except the teacher and possibly the boy who sits behind her, Bill Byron.
- **Wednesday**—The text says that Peggy and Maddie notice that Wanda is absent on Wednesday.

Guided Close Reading—Section 2:
The Dresses Game & A Bright Blue Day
(page 27)
1. Maddie does not like the game. She wishes Peggy would stop teasing Wanda. She feels embarrassed, but she is afraid to speak up.
2. Maddie does not say anything and fiddles with things in her hands.
3. Maddie is worried that Peggy and the other girls will tease her because she is poor and wears handed-down clothes.

Making Connections—Section 2:
The Dresses Game & A Bright Blue Day
(page 28)
The book describes the October day as bright and blue, so drawings should reflect that description. Students' responses for what the weather is like will vary depending on where they live.

Language Learning—Section 2:
The Dresses Game & A Bright Blue Day
(page 29)
- inseparable—underline *in*, match to *not able to separate*
- impatient—underline *im*, match to *not patient*
- unexpected—underline *un*, match to *not what is expected*
- uncomfortable—underline *un*, match to *not comfortable*
1. The word **disorganized** means to be unorganized or messy.

Story Elements—Section 2:
The Dresses Game & A Bright Blue Day
(page 30)

The girls admire Cecile's new dress.
The other girls in the circle begin describing their dresses.
Wanda tells the girls she has a hundred dresses at home.
The girls laugh and make fun of what Wanda has said.
Peggy begins to tease Wanda about the hundred dresses every day by asking her about them.

Vocabulary Activity—Section 3:
The Contest & The Hundred Dresses (page 33)

Nouns	Verbs	Adjectives
trimmings	disguise	lavish
exhibition	recognize	miserable
coward		brilliant

1. Maddie's mom **disguises** her dresses with **trimmings** so the other girls won't notice that they are Peggy's old dresses.

Guided Close Reading—Section 3:
The Contest & The Hundred Dresses (page 36)

1. Maddie has a sick feeling in her stomach because she is thinking about how Wanda has been treated.
2. Maddie decides that she had made Wanda's life miserable by not saying anything to Peggy.
3. Maddie wants to go to Boggins Heights to see if Wanda has moved. She wants to tell Wanda that she has won the contest.

Story Elements—Section 3:
The Contest & The Hundred Dresses (page 39)

- **Maddie**—Maddie doesn't say anything about Wanda's dresses, but she doesn't stop Peggy from teasing either.
- **Peggy**—Peggy doesn't believe Wanda's story about the hundred dresses. She asks her every day about the dresses in a mocking way.
- **Wanda**—Wanda tells the girls that she has a hundred dresses at home in her closet. Peggy keeps asking her about the hundred dresses in a teasing way.

Story Elements—Section 3
The Contest & The Hundred Dresses (page 40)

The classroom is described as having dress designs everywhere, on every surface including: every ledge and windowsill, tacked to the tops of the blackboards, and spread over the bird charts. They are described as "lined up." Drawings should reflect the description.

Guided Close Reading—Section 4:
Up on Boggins Heights (page 45)

1. Maddie decides she is no longer going to stand by and say nothing about someone who is being picked on.
2. Maddie suggests that kids are picked on for being funny looking or because they have strange names.
3. Maddie understands she may lose her friendship with Peggy, but she is willing to in order to do the right thing.

Making Connections—Section 4:
Up on Boggins Heights (page 46)

Definitions will vary, but should be similar to the ones below. Illustrations should show the specified land features.

Land Feature	Definition
hill	a rounded area of land that is higher than the land around it.
brook	a small stream
woods	area of land covered by many trees

Language Learning—Section 4:
Up on Boggins Heights (page 47)

1. afternoon—damp and dismal
2. Boggins Heights—drab and cheerless
3. the cat—yellow and timid
4. the chair—dilapidated and wooden
5. old man Svenson's hair—yellow and tangled

Story Elements—Section 4:
Up on Boggins Heights (page 49)

Answers will vary but may include:

Peggy	Maddie
Peggy wants to go try to find Wanda, but when she and Maddie cannot find her, Peggy is not bothered by it. She states that asking all the questions about the dresses probably gave Wanda ideas for her dress designs.	Maddie is very bothered by not being able to find Wanda. She really wants to try to make things right. Maddie thinks a lot about what has happened and determines not to stand by while other people are being made fun of. She will stand up for them.

Guided Close Reading—Section 5:
The Letter to Room 13 (page 54)

1. The dress design is described as vivid and brilliant with color, so much so that Maddie doesn't even notice the face at first.
2. The drawing is described as having "the same short blonde hair, blue eyes, and wide straight mouth." When she looks at the face, Maddie realizes it is her.
3. Maddie runs over to Peggy's house to look at Peggy's drawing and to share the excitement with Peggy.

Story Elements—Section 5:
The Letter to Room 13 (page 57)

Answers will vary, but settings may include: Christmastime; Miss Mason's classroom; the town described as the girls walk home (grocery store, etc.); Maddie's house/room; Peggy's house/room

Comprehension Assessment (pages 65–66)

1. C. They wait for Wanda, but she never comes.
2. B. They play a game called "the dresses game."
3. A. The dresses are the dresses that Wanda was talking about.
4. Maddie learns that she should stand up for others even if it might mean losing a friend.
5. B. The faces in the drawings are of the two girls'.